Elias Hill
101 Lawyer Jokes For Lawyers
Copyright 2017
Self-published, Tiny Camel Books

Tiny Camel Books
tinycamelbooks.com
tinycamelbooks@gmail.com

101
Lawyer Jokes
For Lawyers

By: Elias Hill

Illustrations By: Katherine Hogan

What do you get if you put 100 clients in your basement?

A whine cellar.

If you think
lawyer jokes
are funny,

next time you're
in trouble call a
comedian.

My friend was telling a lot of lawyer jokes at the party.

My favorite one was when everyone left and she asked me for free advice.

Your only hope is that the jury will suffocate

under all of the evidence against you.

If you cannot afford a lawyer,

this trial will go a lot faster.

What do you call a lawyer with an IQ of 130?

Your Honor. What do you call a lawyer with an IQ of 70?

Senator.

As with any lawsuit you'll go through seven stages of grief:

shock, denial, bargaining, guilt, anger, depression, and bankruptcy.

For his birthday, I bought my son a new set of

class action figures. Courtroom sold seperately.

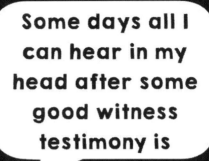

The client who
pays the least,

complains
the most.

I'd like to request a recess, your Honor.

As the witness's pants are on fire.

I got an offer to be an attorney for Ireland's greatest rock band.

But, sorry, I'm not pro Bono.

Then he said, "Your money or your life!"

I told him I never accept the first offer.

What do you specialize in?

Divorce and personal bankruptcy.

Your Honor, it's against my religion to judge others. Only God can do that.

You're excused.

Crazy coincidence, but she just converted me.

Members of the jury,

everything that other guy said is a bunch of lies. Thank you.

On tonight's ripped from reality episode of Cops & Lawyers,

defense lawyer Sophie finds herself in the library reading for fifteen hours.

How does the defendant pleaed?

Like this your Honor, [whiney voice] Noooo, I didn't do it, you guys! I'm serious!

Haha. Do it again.

Your Honor, may I approach the bench?

[whispers] That other guy is being totally mean right now!

How many lawyers does it take to change a lightbulb?

Hourly or flat fee?

My daughter's teacher asked her what comes after a sentence.

She said an appeal.

A good lawyer
knows the law.

A great lawyer
knows the judge.

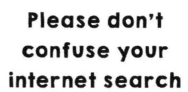

Dance like no one is watching.

But email like it may one day be read aloud in a deposition.

What do you mean you don't recognize me? You sent me to prison!

I wasn't even a judge then.

No, you were my lawyer.

What did your grandmother die of?

You would have to ask her yourself. I'd be speculating if I told you.

My parents lent me $100,000 for my education, and I paid back every penny as soon as I had my first case.

Wow. What sort of case was it?

My parents sued me for the money.

So the bad news is your blood is at the crime scence and the DNA tests prove you did it.

What's the good news?

Your total cholesterol level is only 160.

They say I'm banned from practicing law.

Ha! I'm so good, I don't need to practice.

The only thing preventing me from punching you in the face right now

is my fear of the character and fitness committee.

Being a lawyer is like riding a bike.

Except the bike is on fire and you're on fire. Everything's on fire because you're in hell.

Let's celebrate passing the bar exam,

by doing things that could get us disbarred.

Imitation is the sincerest form of

intellectual property theft.

Never make plans for the day.

Premeditated equals harsher punishment.

Nothing comes easy in life.

Even Santa comes with a clause.

What's
a lawyer's
favorite drink?

A subpoena
colada!

What do you call a smiling, sober, courteous person at a bar association convention?

The caterer.

If a lawyer is talking in a forest and there's no one around to hear her,

can she still bill for it?

Everything I tell you is totally confidential, right? No matter how nefarious?

Uh-oh.

How do you get a group of personal injury lawyers to smile for their picture?

"Say fees!"

I'm leaving my wife, she makes the worst coffee.

Sounds like you have grounds for divorce.

Would you like a bench trial or a jury trial?

Jury trial. I'd rather have 12 ignorant people decide my fate instead of one.

Isn't it true you were given $500 to throw this case?

The witness will answer the question.

Oh, I thought he was talking to you.

Still waiting for the day when I can yell in court,

"You can't handle the truth!"

Any lawyer who says "statue" of limitations instead of "statute,"

deserves to be smacked in the face with one.

"Lying" is such a grim term.

We prefer "testimony without borders."

I heard you think law is confusing.

Let me throw in some Latin to help.

If it takes three years to get there,

it better be one hell of a bar.

The rule against perpetuities provides no interest is good unless it must vest, if at all, not later than twenty-one years after the death of some life in being at the creation of the interest.

The hell?

Remember, the prosecution bears the burden of proof.

And the defense bears the burden of twisting and perverting said truth.

What did the lawyer wear to court?

His lawsuit.

I'm surprised Abraham Lincoln was so honest despite being a lawyer.

It's the politician angle that surprises me.

I'm Gina, but you can call me

Advocatus Diaboli.

If you agree to
pay my fee,

it will also help
bolster your
insanity defense.

Becoming a lawyer is like being pregnant,

everyone says, "Congratulations" but they don't understand the pain.

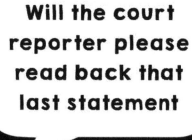

If your lawyer is using a flip phone and wearing a suit that doesn't fit,

you're going to jail.

Fac ut nemo me vocet.

Hold my calls.

When you start hating on lawyers just remember

the 40% who never think of running for office.

Made in the USA
Columbia, SC
15 August 2020

16380706R00059